ACCA
Corporate and Business Law ENG (LW)

Pocket Notes

British library cataloguing-in-publication data

A catalogue record for this book is available from the British Library.

Published by:
Kaplan Publishing UK
Unit 2 The Business Centre
Molly Millars Lane
Wokingham
Berkshire
RG41 2QZ

ISBN 978-1-83735-031-5

© Kaplan Financial Limited, 2025

Printed and bound in Great Britain.

The text in this material and any others made available by any Kaplan Group company does not amount to advice on a particular matter and should not be taken as such. No reliance should be placed on the content as the basis for any investment or other decision or in connection with any advice given to third parties. Please consult your appropriate professional adviser as necessary. Kaplan Publishing Limited and all other Kaplan group companies expressly disclaim all liability to any person in respect of any losses or other claims, whether direct, indirect, incidental, consequential or otherwise arising in relation to the use of such materials.

All rights reserved. No part of this publication may be reproduced, stored in a retrieval system, or transmitted, in any form or by any means, electronic, mechanical, photocopying, recording or otherwise, without the prior written permission of Kaplan Publishing.

Contents

Chapter 1: Essential elements of the legal system 1

Chapter 2: Contract law 13

Chapter 3: The law of torts 27

Chapter 4: Employment law 35

Chapter 5: Agency law 45

Chapter 6: Types of business organisation 49

Chapter 7: Corporations and legal personality 55

Chapter 8: Capital and financing 77

Chapter 9: Directors 91

Chapter 10: Corporate administration 101

Chapter 11: Insolvency 111

Chapter 12: Corporate and fraudulent behaviour 119

Index I.1

Paper background

The aim of ACCA Corporate and Business Law, is to develop knowledge and skills in the understanding of the general legal framework, and of specific legal areas relating to business, recognising the need to seek further specialist legal advice where necessary.

Objectives of the syllabus

- Identify the essential elements of the legal system including the main sources of law.
- Recognise and apply the appropriate legal rules relating to the law of obligations.
- Explain and apply the law relating to employment relationships.
- Distinguish between alternative forms and constitutions of business organisations.
- Recognise and compare types of capital and the financing of companies.
- Describe and explain how companies are managed, administered and regulated.
- Recognise the legal implications relating to insolvency law.
- Demonstrate an understanding of corporate and fraudulent behaviour.

Core areas of the syllabus

- Essential elements of the legal system.
- The law of obligations.
- Employment law.
- The formation and constitution of business organisations.
- Capital and the financing of companies.
- Management, administration and regulation of companies.
- Legal implications relating to insolvency law.
- Corporate fraudulent and criminal behaviour.

Examination Format

The examination is a two-hour assessment – available as a computer-based examination.

The assessment will contain 100% compulsory questions and will comprise the following:

Section A:
- 20 × 1 mark objective test questions
- 25 x 2 mark objective test questions

Section B:
- 5 × 6 mark multi-task questions

Computer-based examination (CBE) tips

Be sure you understand how to use the software before you start the exam. If in doubt, ask the assessment centre staff to explain it to you.

Questions are displayed on the screen and answers are entered using keyboard and mouse. At the end of the exam, you are given a certificate showing the result you have achieved.

Read each question very carefully.

Double-check your answer before committing yourself to it.

Answer every question – If you do not know the answer, you don't lose anything by guessing. Think carefully before you guess.

With a multiple-choice question, eliminate first those answers that you know are wrong. Then choose the most appropriate answer from those that are left.

Remember that only one answer to a multiple-choice question can be right. After you have eliminated the ones that you know to be wrong, if you are still unsure, guess. But only do so after you have double-checked that you have only eliminated answers that are definitely wrong.

Don't panic if you realise you've answered a question incorrectly. Getting one question wrong will not mean the difference between passing and failing.

Quality and accuracy are of the utmost importance to us so if you spot an error in any of our products, please send an email to mykaplanreporting@kaplan.com with full details, or follow the link to the feedback form in MyKaplan.

Our Quality Co-ordinator will work with our technical team to verify the error and take action to ensure it is corrected in future editions.

chapter 1

Essential elements of the legal system

In this chapter

- Definition of law.
- Types of law.
- Criminal law v civil law.
- The main English civil courts.
- The main criminal courts.
- Other courts.
- Sources of law.
- Judicial precedent.
- The hierarchy of the courts.
- Rules of statutory interpretation.
- Human rights law.

Essential elements of the legal system

Definition of law

The principles and regulations established in a community by some authority and applicable to its people whether in the form of legislation or of custom and policies recognised and enforced by judicial decision.

Types of law

Public law	Private law
Deals with matters relating to whole country e.g. criminal law, constitutional law and administrative law.	Deals with law enforced between individuals e.g. contract and family law.

Criminal law v civil law

Criminal law	Civil law
Criminal law relates to conduct which the State considers with disapproval and which it seeks to control.	Civil law is a form of private law and involves the relationships between individual citizens.
Purpose is the enforcement of particular forms of behaviour by the State, which acts to ensure compliance.	Purpose is to settle disputes between individuals and to provide remedies.
In criminal law the case is brought by the State in the name of the Crown. A criminal case will be reported as Rex v ..., where Rex means the latin for 'king'.	In civil law the case is brought by the claimant, who is seeking a rememdy. The case will be referred to by the names of the parties involved in the dispute, such as Brown v Smith.
Burden of proof – on the prosecution.	**Burden of proof** – on the claimant.
Standard of proof – guilt must be shown **beyond reasonable doubt**.	**Standard of proof** – liability must be shown on the **balance of probabilities**.
Object – to regulate society by the threat of punishment.	Object – usually financial compensation to put the claimant in the position they would have been in had the wrong not occurred.
If found guilty the criminal court will sentence the defendant and it may fine them or impose a period of imprisonment. If innocent the accused will be acquitted.	The civil court will order the defendant to pay damages or it may order some other remedy, e.g. specific performance or injunction.

Essential elements of the legal system

The main English civil courts

Supreme Court (previously House of Lords)
Normally 5 Justices hear appeals from Court of Appeal and exceptionally from High Court

Court of Appeal
3 Lords Justices of Appeal hear appeals from the High Court and County Courts

County Court

First instance civil claims in contract, tort, landlord & tenant, probate and insolvency.
1 District judge hears small claims (max £10,000).
1 Circuit judge hears most fast-track cases (£10,000 - £25,000) and some multi-track cases (over £25,000 and/or complex cases).

High Court of Justice

1 High Court judge in first instance. 2-3 for appeals. King's Bench Division hears first instance contract and tort multi-track claims. Chancery Division deals with land law, trusts, company law, partnership law, insolvency, etc. Hears appeals from County Courts on probate & insolvency. Family Division hears matrimonial cases.

Magistrates' court

Jurisdiction is mainly criminal (see section on criminal courts) but does have civil jurisdiction in family matters such as contact orders, adoption, and maintenance. There are also powers of recovery of council tax arrears and charges for water, gas and electricity.

The main criminal courts

Supreme Court (previously House of Lords)
Normally five Justices hear appeals from the Court of Appeal and exceptionally from High Court.

Court of Appeal
Three Lord Justice of Appeal hear appeals from the Crown Court.

Crown Court
Presided over by a judge whose role is to decide questions of law and impose the punishment.
Case will be heard before a jury whose role is to decide questions of fact i.e. whether defendant is guilty of the offence.

Divisional Court of the King's Bench Division
Three judges preside.
Hears appeals from Magistrates Court on points of law.
Appeals go directly to the Supreme Court.

Magistrates Court
Court of first instance. Deals with criminal cases in various ways:
- Summary offences – decides whether defendant is guilty of the offence and imposes the penalty.
- Indictable offences – where there is to be trial by jury. Magistrates pass serious cases to the Crown Court.
- Offences triable either way – the defendant can choose whether to be tried in the Magistrates Court or the Crown Court.

Presided over by either:
- Lay Magistrates. The bench usually consists of three.
- Stipendiary Magistrate sitting alone.
- Appeals on questions of fact go to the Crown Court.
- Case stated appeals on questions of law go to the High Court.

Other courts

European Court of Human Rights	Judicial Committee of the Privy Council
The final court of appeal in relation to matters concerning the Human Rights Act 1998. Must have exhausted proceedings in the English courts before ECtHR will hear case.	The highest court of appeal for a number of Commonwealth countries, crown dependencies and UK overseas territories. Hears both civil and criminal appeals. The right to appeal to the JPC is regulated by the constitution and legislation of the particular country. Proceedings take place in the Supreme Court of the UK.
No appeal.	No appeal.

Sources of law

Case law	Legislation
Common law • Introduced the system of precedent. • The only remedy was damages. • Rigid and inflexible.	**Direct legislation** = Acts of Parliament. A Bill must go through the following stages in both the House of Lords and the House of Commons: 1st reading, 2nd reading, committee stage, report stage, 3rd reading, Royal Assent.
Equity • Began as a form of appeal. • More flexible than the common law. • Introduced new discretionary remedies such as injunctions and specific performance. • Concerned with fairness. Equitable remedies are not available as of right. Must meet the **maxims of equity**: e.g. • He who seeks equity must have acted equitably; and • delay defeats equity.	**Indirect legislation** = delegated legislation. Consists of: • **Statutory instruments** – Made by Government Ministers using powers delegated by Parliament • **Bye-laws** – Made by local authorities • **Orders in Council** – Made by the Privy Council in the name of the Monarch on the advice of the Prime Minister.

Judicial precedent

Ratio decidendi	Obiter dicta
The legal reason for the decision	Statements which are not part of the ratio
The ratio is capable of forming the binding precedent	Persuasive rather than binding precedent

The hierarchy of the courts

Supreme Court – Binds all lower courts. From 1966 does not bind itself.

Court of Appeal – Binds all lower courts and itself unless earlier decision overruled or inconsistent with European law. Not bound by own criminal decisions.

High Court – Not bound by its own decisions, but strong persuasive authority.

Advantages of judicial precedent – consistency, flexibility, practical.

Disadvantages – complex, restricts judges' discretion. However, judges retain discretion by 'distinguishing on the facts' or overruling lower courts.

Rules of statutory interpretation

Literal rule	Golden rule	Mischief rule	Purposive Rule
Words must be given their ordinary grammatical meaning, even if it produces an undesirable outcome.	Used where the literal rule gives more than one meaning or provides an absurd result. Involves choosing the meaning that produces the least absurd result.	Used to interpret a statute in a way which provides a remedy for the mischief the statute was enacted to prevent.	This is a more modern approach. Here the court is not just looking to see what the gap was in the old law, it is making a decision as to what they felt Parliament meant to achieve.
Fisher v Bell – It was a criminal offence to 'offer for sale' a flick-knife. A shopkeeper who displayed one in his shop window was held not guilty as the court chose to follow the contract law meaning of the word 'offer'.	**Adler v George** – The words 'in the vicinity of' a prohibited place' in the Official Secrets Act were held to cover the acts of the defendant which took place 'within' a prohibited place.	**Gorris v Scott** – As the purpose of the statute was to prevent the spread of contagious disease and not guard against the danger of the property being washed overboard, the claim failed.	**Gardiner v Sevenoaks RDC (1950)** – The purpose of the Act was to protect the safety of persons working in all places where film was stored. If film was stored in a cave, the word 'premises' included the cave.

Note also – **Euisdem generis** – general words mean the same kind of thing as the specific words they follow. **Expressio unio est exclusio alterius** – a statute which expresses particular things by implication excludes everything else.

Human Rights Law

What are human rights?	These are the basic rights and freedoms that belong to every person in the world.
	The purpose is to give individuals protection in their everyday life such as the right to freedom of religion and belief and the right to respect for private and family life.
The law	These have developed over the years such as the development of the Universal Declaration of Human Rights which followed the Second World War.
	In the UK the Human Rights Act 1998 sets out the fundamental rights and freedoms that everyone in the UK is entitled to.

Essential elements of the legal system

chapter

2

Contract law

In this chapter

- Offer.
- Acceptance.
- Consideration.
- The part-payment problem.
- Privity of contract.
- Intention to create legal relations.
- Terms.
- Exclusion clauses.
- Breach of contract.
- Remedies for breach of contract.

Offer

Definition

An offer is a definite and unequivocal statement of willingness to be bound on specified terms without further negotiations. Once accepted it forms a valid contract.

It can be made to a particular person, to a class of persons or even to the whole world: **Carlill v Carbolic Smoke Ball Co**.

What is not an offer?

- A mere statement of selling price in response to a request for info.
- An invitation to treat = an invitation to the other party to make an offer; e.g. **Gibson v Manchester City Council**: 'we may be prepared to sell'.

Examples of invitations to treat

- Most adverts – **Partridge v Crittenden** (advert for rare birds).
- Shop window displays – **Fisher v Bell** (flick-knives).
- Goods on shop shelves – **Pharmaceutical Society of GB v Boots**.
- Tenders.

How does an offer terminate?

- **Revocation** by the offeror at any time before acceptance, even if agreed to keep open. However, must be communicated to offeree by offeror or reliable third party.
- **Rejection** by the offeree – either outright or by a counter-offer – **Hyde v Wrench**.
- **Lapse** – on death of offeror or offeree, the failure of a condition or after expiry of fixed time.
- Failure of a pre-condition.

Acceptance

> **Definition**

Acceptance is the unqualified and unconditional assent to all the terms of an offer. It can be oral, written or by conduct: **Carlill v Carbolic Smoke Ball Co**.

Communication

- Acceptance is not effective until communicated to offeror – **Entores v Miles Far Eastern**.
- Offeror can stipulate particular mode of acceptance. However, if merely requests a mode, offeree not limited to that mode.
- Offeror can't stipulate that silence is acceptance – **Felthouse v Bindley**.
- Offeror can expressly or impliedly dispense with need for communication.

The postal rule

- An exception to the general rule that acceptance must be communicated.
- Acceptance is complete as soon as letter posted – **Adams v Lindsell**.
- Postal rule applies even if letter never received – **Household Fire Insurance v Grant**.
- Only applies if letter properly stamped and addressed and if post is reasonable method of communication.
- Does not apply if offeror states he must actually receive the acceptance.

Consideration

Definition

'Consideration is an act or forbearance (or the promise of it) on the part of one party to a contract as the price of the promise made to him by the other party to the contract' – **Dunlop v Selfridge**.

'Some right, interest, profit or benefit accruing to one party, or some forbearance, detriment, loss or responsibility given, suffered or undertaken by the other' – **Currie v Misa**.

Types of consideration

- Executory consideration is given where there is an exchange of promises to do something in the future.
- Executed consideration means that the consideration is in the form of an act carried out at the time the contract is made.
- Past consideration – this is an act which has been wholly performed before the other party gives his promise. It is insufficient and therefore is not valid.

General rule	Consideration must not be past
Re McArdle	Husband & wife repaired house. Held work could not support a later promise to reimburse the cost.
Re Casey's Patents	Exception – a request for services may be treated as an implied promise to pay, even if actual promise not made until later.

General rule	**Consideration must be sufficient but need not be adequate**
Chappell & Co. v Nestlé	Records sold for 1s 6d plus 3 chocolate wrappers. Wrappers were part of the consideration even though they had minimal value.
Thomas v Thomas	Promise to convey house to widow for rent of £1 a year was binding. The consideration had value, even though inadequate.
White v Bluett	Son's promise to stop complaining did not amount to consideration as not valuable.
General rule	**Performance of an existing statutory duty is not consideration**
Collins v Godefroy	A witness was promised payment if he would attend court and give evidence. No consideration as legally required to attend court.
Glasbrook Bros. v Glamorgan CC	Exception – action exceeding statutory duty is consideration. Company required the police to provide protection in excess of statutory requirement. Held: police had provided sufficient consideration to give entitlement to remuneration.
General rule	**Performance of existing contractual duty is not consideration**
Stilk v Myrick	Captain promised to share wages of deserting seamen with rest of crew. Not binding as no extra consideration from seamen.
Williams v Roffey Bros.	Exception – R offered W extra money to complete work on time. Although W did no extra work, held sufficient consideration as enabled R to avoid penalty clause. Also, no pressure by W to make R offer the extra money.

The part-payment problem

The rule in Pinnel's case – states that payment of a lesser sum, in satisfaction of a greater sum, cannot be satisfaction for the whole sum.

Exceptions

- Variation of terms at the creditor's request (with accord and satisfaction).

E.g. payment on an earlier date.

- Part-payment by a third party.
- Equitable doctrine of promissory estoppel prevents a person going back on his promise to accept a lesser amount – **Central London Property Trust v High Tree House**.

Limitations on promissory estoppel:

- It is a 'shield not a sword', i.e. it can only be used as a defence.
- It may only have suspensory effect, i.e. if give notice, can insist on future payments in full.
- 'He who comes to equity must come with clean hands', i.e. party seeking to rely on promissory estoppel must have acted fairly.

Privity of contract

The general rule	Only the parties to a contract: • acquire rights and obligations under it • can sue and be sued on it.
Exceptions	The Contracts (Rights of Third Parties) Act 1999 where a third party is identified.
	A collateral contract between one of the parties and a third party relating to the same subject matter (**Shanklin Pier v Detel Products**).
	Restrictive covenants in relation to land law (**Tulk v Moxhay**).
	Insurance law allows a third party to take benefit of a contract of insurance.
	Trust law allows a beneficiary to enforce a trust.
	Agency law allows an agent to make a contract between his principal and a third party.
	An executor can enforce contracts made by the deceased for whom he is acting.

Intention to create legal relations

A contract does not exist unless the parties intend it to be legally enforceable. The law presumes the intention of the parties based on the type of agreement. The presumption can be rebutted by clear evidence to the contrary.

Domestic or social agreements	Commercial agreements
Presume no intention to be legally bound	Presume intention to be legally bound
Balfour v Balfour – Husband promised wife monthly allowance. Not legally binding as domestic arrangement.	**Jones v Vernon's Pools** – Wording of contract stated 'binding in honour only'. Therefore no intention to be legally bound.
Simpkins v Pays – Competition entry between Pays, granddaughter and lodger. Presumption rebutted as clearly intended to share prize money.	
Merritt v Merritt – Presumption rebutted as husband and wife separated.	

Terms

Terms v representations – A representation is something that is said by the offeror in order to induce the offeree to enter into the contract. It may or may not become a term of that contract.

Types of terms

Conditions	Warranties	Innominate terms
An important term going to the root of the contract.	Less important term, incidental to main purpose.	Indeterminate – neither a condition nor a warranty.
Breach can result in damages or discharge.	Breach results in damages only.	Remedy depends on effects of breach.
Poussard v Spiers – opera singer failed to appear on opening night. Held: breach of condition entitling injured party to treat contract as ended.	**Bettini v Gye** – opera singer failed to attend rehearsals. Held: breach of warranty. Injured party could not treat contract as ended. Damages only.	**The Hansa Nord** – some of ship's cargo arrived in poor condition. Buyer rejected whole cargo. Held: only remedy was damages. Breach insufficient to justify treating contract as ended.

Sources of terms

Express – contained in contract; written or oral.
Implied – by statute, by the courts if necessary to give business efficacy, by the nature of the contract, by custom and usage.

Exclusion clauses

Definition

A term that seeks to exclude a party's liability for breach of contract.

Common law rules	
Must be incorporated into contract – by signature, notice or previous dealings.	
L'Estrange v Graucob	Clause incorporated by **signature**, even if the signatory did not read or understand the document.
Curtis v Chemical Cleaning	**Exception** – signature does not incorporate clause if effect of term was misrepresented. Liability for damage to wedding dress not excluded due to misrepresentation of clause.
Olley v Marlborough Court	Clause incorporated by **notice**, provided given **before making the contract**. Notice in hotel room did not exclude liability as contract made at reception desk.
Spurling v Bradshaw	Clause incorporated by **consistent course of dealings** between parties on terms which included exclusion clause.
Hollier v Rambler Motors	Three or four deals between a garage and private customer over a five-year period insufficient to constitute course of dealing.

Wording must cover loss – contra proferentum rule interprets clause narrowly	
Photo Productions Ltd. v Securicor	Contract to provide security for factory excluded liability for 'any injurious act or default by any employee'. Security guard burned factory down. Clause valid as wording unambiguous.

Contract law

```
Does the clause pass the common law rules? If no, the
clause is void. If yes, consider statutory rules.
```

- If the contract is made in the course of business, UCTA 1977 applies.
  - Void if exempts liability for death or personal injury.
  - Other loss – void unless 'reasonable'.

- If one party is a consumer and the other is in business, CRA 2015 applies.
  - Unfair (and not binding) if not expressed in plain language or if it causes an imbalance in parties' rights to the detriment of the consumer.

Breach of contract

Definition – Breach of contract occurs where one of the parties fails to carry out the terms of the contract in the manner required by the contract.

Actual breach	• becomes apparent at or after the time set for performance.
Anticipatory breach	• occurs before performance. • may be **express**, e.g. one party declares they have no intention of performing the contract. • may be **implied**, e.g. one party does something which makes performance impossible. • the innocent party can choose to wait until the due date for performance before taking action. However, he runs the risk of the contract being discharged for some other reason.

Consequences of breach

Damages	• available for breach of any contract.
Treat contract as discharged	• available for breach of condition or where other party has made an anticipatory breach.

Remedies for breach of contract

Damages

- Common law remedy. Available as of right for breach of contract.
- Aim to put injured party in position would have been in if contract properly performed.
- Intended to be compensatory not punitive.

Remoteness of loss

Hadley v Baxendale	General damages arise naturally from the breach. Special damages do not occur in the normal course of things, but were reasonably in the contemplation of the parties, at the time they made the contract, as the probable result of the breach.
Victoria Laundries v Newman	Delay in delivery of boiler caused loss of normal trading profit, plus an extra large profit on the loss of a government contract. Held: could recover damages for first loss, but not second as unknown to defendant i.e. too remote.

chapter 3

The law of torts

In this chapter

- Tort.
- Tort of negligence.
- Negligence by professionals.
- The tort of 'passing off'.

Tort

Definition

A tort is a type of civil wrong: e.g. negligence, trespass. It is a breach of a legal duty or infringement of a legal right which gives rise to a claim for damages. For an action for negligence to succeed, the claimant must show three things, that:

Tort of negligence

- A duty of care was owed to them by the defendant.

- There was a breach of that duty.

- The resulting damage was principally caused by the negligence.

Duty of care

- The existence of a duty of care is a question of law.
- One owes a duty of care to one's neighbour **(Donoghue v Stevenson)**.

Definition of neighbour

'...persons who are so directly affected by my act that I ought reasonably to have them in contemplation'.

The limits of the duty of care

In the case of The Nicholas H (Marc Rich & Co v Bishops Rock Marine) (1995), four tests were laid down which should be followed in determining whether a duty of care exists.

The issues to be considered are:

- Was the damage reasonably foreseeable by the defendant at the time of the act or omission?
- Is there a neighbourhood principle or sufficient proximity (closeness) between the parties?
- Should the law impose a duty of care between the parties i.e. is it fair and reasonable to do so?
- Is there a matter of public policy which exists or requires that no duty of care should exist?

The Nicholas H case focused on financial loss, but these tests should also be applied when determining the duty of care for physical damage cases.

Breach of that duty

- Normally the claimant must show that the defendant has been negligent. The test is that of the 'reasonable man' (**Blyth v Birmingham Waterworks Co**).
- Lack of skill is no defence.
- There is no negligence if reasonable precautions have been taken.
- The courts do take the surrounding circumstances into account.

Resulting damage

- The damage must be a direct consequence of the negligence. If the accident would have occurred anyway, the causal link is not established.
- The damage must have been reasonably foreseeable at the time of the negligence. It must not be too remote.

Negligence by professionals

Hedley Byrne v Heller established that a professional person owes a duty of care to any person he knew or reasonably ought to have known would rely on his professional statement. Liability is only owed when:

- the proximity test is satisfied. The defendant must have known that the information would be communicated to the claimant, used for a particular purpose and relied upon by the claimant
- the floodgate test applies. The courts will only make the defendant liable when it is reasonable to do so in the public interest.

Caparo Industries v Dickman applied the proximity and floodgate tests to auditors and held that the auditor is not liable to third parties.

When the auditor gives his audit report to the shareholders he is fulfilling a statutory role and it would be unreasonable to make him liable to anyone other than the shareholders as a body. So if he is negligent only the company can sue him. Individual shareholders and third parties cannot.

However if the auditor gives specific assurances to a third party, he is liable to that third party if the assurance is given negligently.

An accountant is expected to follow the requirements of accounting standards and the code of conduct of his professional body.

In **JEB Fasteners v Marks, Bloom & Co.** accountants were held to be negligent for not following normal accountancy practice.

Defences

Contributory negligence	The court may reduce any damages it awards to the claimant, depending on the degree to which he is judged responsible for his own loss.
Volenti non fit injuria	If a person has freely consented to a negligent act he cannot obtain a remedy.
Novus actus interveniens	Where there is a new intervening act this may break the chain of causation removing liability from the defendant. There are three types of intervening acts: • Act of the claimant • Act of a third party • Natural events
Exclusion clauses	If valid is a viable defence. But need to consider if it falls within the provision of the Consumer Rights Act 2015.
Act of God	Liability is excluded if the act occurred in the course of nature i.e. it was an 'act of god'.

The tort of 'passing off'

The tort arises:
- where one business uses a name which is similar to that of an existing business; and
- it misleads persons into believing that they are the same business; and
- it causes actual damage to that business or will probably do so.

Remedy

If proved, the court may restrain the business from trading under that name and order that damages be paid to the person whose business has suffered loss.

Ewing v Buttercup Margarine Company

Ewing owned the well-known Buttercup Dairy Company. He succeeded in restraining the Buttercup Margarine Company from using that name. The court held that the word 'Buttercup' was so closely associated with Ewing dairy products as to be likely to cause confusion if used by the similar, but unconnected, margarine business.

If a company feels than another company has a name which is too similar to its own, it may object to the Company Name Adjudicator under CA 06. The Adjudicator will consider the case and then make their decision. In most cases the Adjudicator will require a name change, and in some cases the Adjudicator may state the new company name.

chapter 4

Employment law

In this chapter

- Employed v self-employed.
- Common law duties.
- Wrongful dismissal.
- Unfair dismissal.
- Constructive dismissal.
- Redundancy.
- Remedies.

Employed v self-employed

Employee	Independent contractor
Works under a contract of service	Works under a contract for services
• **control test** (old) – employee is subject to control by employer as to how, where and when he does his work: **Yewens v Noakes** • integration test = employee if work is integrated into business, not merely accessory	• economic reality test – (multiple test): Worker is in business on own account if he provides own tools, is able to delegate, works for a number of clients, suffers a degree of financial risk as hours and payment are irregular, etc. **Ready Mixed Concrete v Ministry of Pensions**
Importance of difference	

- employees receive statutory protection (e.g. unfair dismissal/redundancy)
- implied terms in contract of employment (e.g. duty of obedience)
- vicarious liability only applies to acts of employees
- insolvency – employee is preferential creditor; self-employed is ordinary unsecured creditor
- pay of employees is net of income tax and national insurance under PAYE system
- state benefits (e.g. statutory sick pay) only available to employees

Common law duties

Duties of employee	Duties of employer
• **Obey lawful and reasonable orders.** **Pepper v Webb.** A gardener refused to plant the plants when instructed by the employer. **Held**: He was in breach of the duty of obedience and this, coupled with the fact that he was rude and surly, justified summary dismissal. • **Exercise care and skill** (indemnify employer if failure causes him loss). • Perform duties personally. • Act in good faith (honest/faithful service) – i.e. not make secret profit/misappropriate property; not compete with the employer; not disclose confidential information or trade secrets: **Hivac v Park Royal Scientific.** • Act in reasonable manner. • Mutual co-operation, trust and confidence.	• **Pay agreed wages** (whether work available or not). • **Indemnify employee** for liabilities properly incurred. • **Take reasonable care for safety** of employee. Case law establishes that this includes safe plant/machinery; safe system of work; competent/safe staff. • Mutual co-operation, trust and confidence. **No duty to provide work.** Exceptionally, duty if: • payment by commission or piece-work. • rely on publicity or need to maintain skill. **No duty to provide references** (but if do so, must be truthful).

Wrongful dismissal

Definition	Minimum notice periods
Employer terminates contract without proper notice or during fixed term (i.e. breach of contract). **Summary dismissal** = no notice.	Continuous employment — Period of notice 1 month – 2 years — 1 week 2 – 12 years — 1 week per year 12 years + — 12 weeks
Summary dismissal is usually wrongful dismissal unless: - employee waives rights or accepts **payment in lieu of notice**. - employee repudiated contract himself or in **fundamental breach** (e.g. wilful refusal to obey orders; failure to show professed skill; serious negligence; breach of duty of good faith).	**Employees' remedies** Sue in the County Court or High Court for damages: - usually receive wages for period of notice - may be additional damages - duty to mitigate loss - specific performance generally not granted.

Unfair dismissal

Definition

- Must be continuously employed for two years. Serve grievance notice on employer.
- **Claim** to Employment Tribunal within **three months** of dismissal.
- Employee must **prove** he was **dismissed**. (If does so, presumed unfair).
- **Employer** must **prove reason** for dismissal is permitted.
- The tribunal must be satisfied that the employer acted reasonably.
- If unfair, entitled to reinstatement, re-engagement or compensation.

Types of dismissal: s.136 ERA 1996

Contract terminated by employer with or without notice.

Fixed-term contract expired and not renewed.

Constructive dismissal.

Statutory fair reasons for dismissal	Inadmissible reasons for dismissal
• Capabilities/qualifications of employee.	• Victimisation of health and safety complainants.
• Conduct of employee.	• Pregnancy or childbirth.
• Redundancy.	• Trade union membership/non-membership/activities.
• Continued employment would contravene statute.	• Assertion of a statutory right.
• Some other substantial reason.	↓
↓	Dismissal for one of these reasons is **automatically unfair**.
Dismissal for one of these reasons is **fair unless employer acted unreasonably** in dismissing for the reason given.	No need to meet length of employment condition.
Must follow proper dismissal procedure.	Additional award of compensation.

Constructive dismissal

Definition	The **employee terminates the contract** with, or without, notice in circumstances which are such that he or she is entitled to terminate it without notice **by reason of the employer's conduct**.
Western Excavating Ltd v Sharp	The employer must be guilty of conduct which is a **significant breach going to the root of the contract** of employment.
Cox Toner (International) Ltd v Crook	If the employee does not resign in the event of the breach, he is deemed to have accepted the breach and waived any rights. However, he need not resign immediately, but may wait until he has found another job.
O'Brien v Associated Fire Alarms	The movement of an employer to a **new location** will normally give rise to a redundancy claim for an employee who does not wish to move, unless his contract contains an **express mobility clause**. Held the employee could resign and claim constructive dismissal.
Simmonds v Dowty Seals Ltd	S had been employed to work on the night shift. When his employer attempted to force him to work on the day shift he resigned. Held: constructively dismissed because the employer had attempt to unilaterally change an express term of the employment contract.

Redundancy

Definition – Under s139(1) Employment Rights Act 1996, an employee is redundant if their dismissal is wholly or mainly attributable to the fact that:

- their employer has ceased, or intends to cease, business; or
- the employer's need for employees to do work of that particular kind has ceased or diminished.

The work may have ceased altogether or only in the place where the employee was employed.

Procedure:

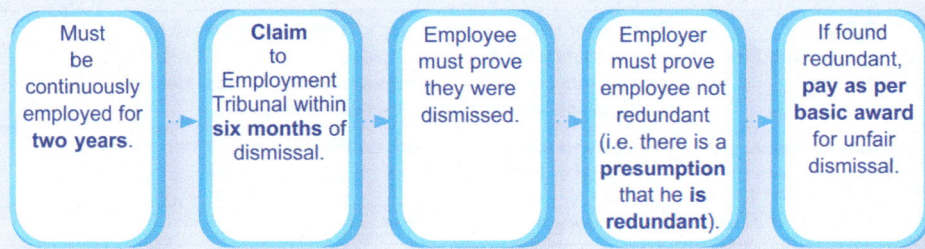

Remedies

Reinstatement	Re-engagement	Compensation
Employee treated as if not dismissed. Returned to same job with no loss of seniority. Only awarded if applicant wishes and if is practicable.	Comparable employment. Employer's failure to comply with reinstatement or re-engagement results in compensation.	Basic award – as for redundancy. Compensatory – max £115,115. Reduced if complainant contributed to their dismissal.

	Calculation of	Redundancy pay/basic award
Not entitled to redundancy payment if unreasonably refused offer of fresh employment (made before old contract expires) to start within four weeks on same or suitable terms.	18-21 years of age	½ week's pay for each year of service
	22-40 years of age	1 week's pay for each year of service
	41 years plus	1½ week's pay for each year of service
		Maximum is for 20 years' service at £700 per week.

chapter 5

Agency law

In this chapter

- How the agency relationship arises.
- Authority.
- Liability of the parties.

How the agency relationship arises

Definition

An agent (A) is a person who is authorised to act for another, the principal (P), in the making of legal relations with third parties. The relationship can arise in a number of ways:

Express agreement	The agreement can be made orally or in writing.
Implied agreement	The agreement can be implied from the parties' conduct.
Necessity	This requires four conditions to be satisfied: • P's property is entrusted to A • an emergency arises making it necessary for A to act • it is not possible to communicate with P • A acts in the interest of P.
Ratification	This requires P to: • have the contractual capacity to make the contract • have been in existence when the contract was made • be identified when the contract is made • be aware of all the material facts • ratify the whole contract within a reasonable time. **NB A void or illegal contract cannot be ratified.**
Estoppel	This arises where P implies that A is his agent. They are then prevented from denying A's authority – **Freeman & Lockyer v Buckhurst Park Properties**.

Authority

Express	This is authority that P has explicitly given to A.
Implied	An agent has implied authority to do things which: • are reasonably incidental to the performance of an expressly authorised act • an agent occupying that position would usually have authority to do • have not been expressly prohibited by P.
Apparent	Such authority arises where A is held out by P as having authority. The representation by P may arise from: • previous dealings (allowing A to make contracts in the past is a representation that A has authority to continue to do so in the future). However, a third party cannot rely on apparent authority when they know of the lack of actual authority.

Liability of the parties

A's fiduciary duty to P:

- A must not allow a personal interest to conflict with that of P
- A must always act in P's best interests
- A must not make a secret profit
- A has a duty to account to P for all money and property received.

Remedies for breach of fiduciary duty:

- P can repudiate the contract with the third party
- A can be dismissed without notice
- P can refuse to pay any money owed to A or recover any money already paid
- P can recover any secret profit made or any bribe.

Disclosed principal – contract is between P and third party. A is not liable or entitled under the contract, unless:

- P is fictitious
- A signs contract in own name
- A refuses to name P
- trade custom dictates personal liability.

Undisclosed principal – when a third party discovers the existence of P he can elect to treat P or A as bound by the transaction.

P's liability to A:

The agent has the right:

- To claim remuneration or commission for services performed
- To claim an indemnity against P for all expenses reasonably incurred in carrying out his obligations
- To exercise a lien over P's property.

chapter 6

Types of business organisation

In this chapter

- Different types of business organisation.
- Authority.

Different types of business organisation

| Sole trader | - The owner 'is' the business – owns the assets and is liable for all the debts.
- No legal formalities are required to set up a sole trader business.
- This form of business is inappropriate for large businesses or those involving a degree of risk. |
|---|---|
| Partnership | Defined by Partnership Act 1890 as the relationship which subsists between persons carrying on a business in common with a view of profit (see below). |
| Limited liability partnership | - An artificial legal entity with perpetual succession. It can hold property in its own right, enter into contracts in its own name, create floating charges, sue and be sued.
- The liability of the members of a limited liability partnership (LLP) is limited to the amount of capital they have agreed to contribute.
- The LLP must file annual accounts and an annual report with Companies House. |
| Company | A corporation is an artificial legal person (see chapter 7). |

Definition

A partnership is a relationship which subsists between two or more persons carrying on a business in common with a view to profit.

Types of partners	Types of partnership
• **General partner** – actively involved in the day-to-day business. • **Sleeping partner** – takes no active part in the running of the business. • **Limited partner in a limited partnership** – contributes specific amount of capital. Liability limited to that amount. Can't take part in the management of the firm. • **Salaried partner** – will receive a fixed amount in income. Not a real partner unless he also receives a share of the profits.	• **Partnership** – governed by Partnership Act 1890. Default position if a partnership is not formed under either of the two Acts below. • **Limited partnership** – governed by Limited Partnership Act 1907. There must be at least one partner with unlimited liability. • **Limited liability partnership** – governed by Limited Liability Partnerships Act 2000. Legally separate from its members.

Authority

The partnership agreement is a contract. Partners are subject to the rules of agency when dealing with each other and on behalf of the business.

Actual authority is the authority P has agreed that A should have. It can be:

- express authority which is set out in the agreement between P and A; or
- implied authority. This is where the terms of A's authority are ambiguous or A is given a discretion to act. The law implies authority to enable A to carry out his express duties.

Apparent authority is the authority of A as it appears to others. Can arise from:

- previous dealings.

Partners are presumed to have authority to buy and sell goods, engage employees, receive payments of debts due to the firm, and engage a solicitor. Trading partnerships are also presumed to be able borrow money.

Watteau v Fenwick – innkeeper continued to have authority to purchase cigars even though new owners had ordered him not to.

Liability of partners	Dissolution of partnership
Every partner is **jointly and severally liable** for any debts and contracts of the business. Outsiders can sue one partner alone or the firm.	• **Without court order** – On expiry of a fixed term or the completion of a specific enterprise.
A **new partner** is not personally liable for anything done before they became a partner.	– One of the partners gives notice. – Death or bankruptcy of a partner.
A **retiring partner** remains liable for debts due at time of retirement. If no notice of retirement is given, firm bound by their actions as still being 'held out' as a partner. Where a third party deals with a partnership after **a change in partners**, all partners of the old firm are still treated as partners until the third party receives notice of the change (e.g. by notice in the Gazette).	• **By Court Order** – Partner has mental disorder or permanent incapacity. – Partner guilty of misconduct. – Partner persistently breaches the partnership agreement. – Business can only be carried on at a loss. – It is just and equitable to do so.

Types of business organisation

chapter 7

Corporations and legal personality

In this chapter

- Veil of incorporation.
- Lifting the veil.
- Limited Liability Partnerships Act.
- Company v partnership.
- Types of company.
- Public company v private company.
- Promoters.
- Pre-incorporation contracts.
- Registration.
- Name of company.
- Articles of association.
- Registers.
- Accounting records and annual return.

Exam focus

This chapter introduces company law as a topic and is fundamental. Company law is the largest area of the syllabus.

Veil of incorporation

Meaning	Company is separate legal entity (i.e. separate from its shareholders).
Consequences	• Company is liable for its own debts. If it fails, liability of the shareholders is limited to any amount still unpaid on their share capital. • Company has perpetual succession, irrespective of fate of shareholders. • Separation of management from ownership.
Salomon v Salomon & Co Ltd	**Facts:** S transferred his business to a limited company. He was majority shareholder and a secured creditor. Company went into liquidation. Other creditors tried to obtain repayment from S personally. **Held:** S as shareholder and director had no personal liability to creditors and he could be repaid in priority as a secured creditor. This enshrined the concepts of separate legal personality and limited liability in the law.
Lee v Lee's Air Farming	**Facts:** Proprietor of a company (also MD and sole employee) was killed in the course of his employment. Liquidator tried to avoid paying compensation to widow on grounds he was not a separate entity from the company. **Held:** The individual and the company were two separate entities, and the company was liable to pay the compensation.
Macaura v Northern Life Assurance	**Facts:** M sold forest to company he formed, but failed to transfer insurance policy into company's name. Forest was destroyed by fire. **Held:** M unable to claim insurance as the company owned the forest, not him, and company unable to claim since it did not have the insurance policy.

Lifting the veil

'Lifting the veil' allows the courts to look at the identity of the shareholders.

Usual result – members or directors become personally liable for the company's debts.

Examples

- If a public company starts to trade without first obtaining a trading certificate, the directors can be made personally liable for any loss or damage suffered by a third party: S767 CA06.
- Under the Company Directors Disqualification Act 1986, if a director who is disqualified participates in the management of a company, that director will be jointly or severally liable for the company's debts.
- Under Insolvency Act 1986 ('IA86'), members and/or directors found to have carried out **wrongful or fraudulent trading** may be personally liable for losses arising as a result.
- A parent company must prepare **group accounts**, consolidating balance sheets and profit and loss accounts of it and its subsidiaries, allowing investors (and others) to judge the financial position of group as a whole.
- Veil only lifted where '**special circumstances** exist indicating that it is a mere facade concealing the true facts' – **Woolfson v Strathclyde Regional Council**.
- **Sham company: Gilford v Horne** – H formed company to run it in competition with G. H had a personal contract with G restraining competition. **Held:** company could be restrained from competition, as H had set it up to evade his own legal obligations.

Limited Liability Partnerships Act

Incorporation	• Incorporation document must be delivered to Registrar stating name of LLP, location and address of registered office, names and addresses of members (minimum two). • Must send a Declaration of Compliance that LLP satisfies requirements of the Limited Liability Partnerships Act 2000. • Registrar issues a certificate of incorporation.
Membership	• First members sign incorporation document. Later members join by agreement with existing members. • Membership ceases on death, dissolution or in accordance with agreement with other members. • Rights and duties are set out in membership agreement. If no agreement, governed by Limited Liability Partnership Regulations 2001. • Each member acts as an agent of the LLP.
Designated members	• Perform the administrative and filing duties of the LLP. • Incorporation document specifies who they are. • Must be at least two designated members. If there are none, all members will be designated members.

Name	• Must end with Limited Liability Partnership, llp or LLP. • Rules on choice are the same as for companies.
Taxation	• Members are treated as if they are partners carrying on business in a partnership, i.e. pay income tax not corporation tax.
Registers	• Register of members • Registers of members usual residential addresses • Register of people with significant control The LLP can keep these registers at its registered office or choose to send the information to the Registrar of Companies to be kept on the public register at Companies House.
Liability for debts	• The liability of a member of an LLP to contribute to its debts is limited to his capital contribution. However, there is no requirement for a capital contribution, and any contribution made can be withdrawn at any time. • The fraudulent and wrongful trading provisions of the Insolvency Act 1986 apply to members of LLPs in the same way as they apply to directors of companies.
Differences between LLP & partnership	• Liability of LLP members is limited to the amount of capital they have agreed to contribute. • The LLP must file annual accounts and an annual report with Companies House. • LLP is an artificial legal entity with perpetual succession. It can hold property in its own right, enter into contracts in its own name, create floating charges, sue and be sued.

Company v partnership

Company	Partnership
Created by registration – with written constitution.	No special formality required to create.
Separate legal person, i.e. can own property, sue or be sued, and contract in own name.	Not a separate legal person – partners own property, are liable on contracts and liable if sued.
Shares transferable.	Limits on transfer of share (may require dissolution of partnership to enable a partner to realise his share).
Can create both fixed and floating charges.	Can only create fixed charges.
Managed by directors, who may or may not also be shareholders.	Managed by partners, who are also the owners of the business.
Company liable for its debts (no personal liability for shareholders).	Partners personally liable for debts of firm.
Must make information about financial affairs and ownership publicly available.	Private business. No disclosure of results.
Companies pay corporation tax.	Partners pay income tax.
Formal dissolution procedure.	May dissolve by agreement.

Types of company

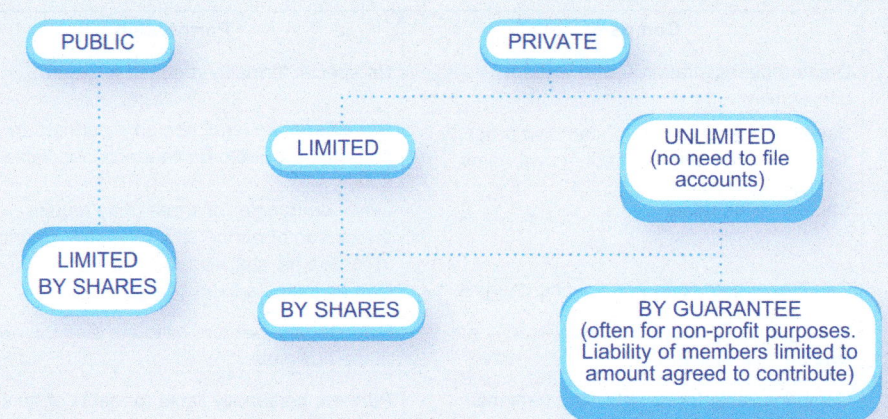

Public company v private company

	Public companies	**Private (limited) companies**
Definition	Registered as a public company.	Any company that is not a public company.
Name	Ends with plc or public limited company.	Ends with Ltd or limited.
Capital	Not less than the authorised minimum (currently £50,000) and, in order to trade, must have allotted shares of at least that amount.	No minimum (or maximum) requirements.
Raising capital	May raise capital by advertising its securities (shares and debentures) as available for public subscription.	Prohibited from offering its securities to the public.
Start of trading	Must obtain trading certificate from Registrar before commence trading.	Can begin from date of incorporation.

Directors	Minimum two.	Minimum one.
Secretary	Must be qualified. Must have one.	Need not have one.
Accounts	Must file accounts within six months of financial year end.	Need not lay accounts before general meeting. Must file within nine months of year end.
Audit	Accounts must be audited.	Audit not required if meets exemption criteria.
AGM	Must be held each year.	Need not hold an AGM
Resolutions	Cannot pass written resolutions.	Can pass written resolutions.

Promoters

Definition	No statutory definition.
	Case law: one who has intention and takes necessary steps to form company. (**Twycross v Grant**). Excludes people acting in professional capacity.
Duties	• Use reasonable care and skill.
	• Disclose any interest in transactions to company and not make 'secret profit'.
	• Disclose any benefit acquired to independent board/ shareholders.
Remedies for non-disclosure	• Rescind contract – but not always possible e.g. if third party rights accrued.
	• Damages – prove loss by company.
	• Recover profit – prove failure to disclose profit from transaction.

Pre-incorporation contracts

Definition

A contract made by a person acting on behalf of an unformed company.

Position at common law – A company, prior to its incorporation, does not have contractual capacity and the promoter is personally liable.

Kelner v Baxter – Promoter liable for unpaid goods, even though they were used by the company.

s51 CA06 – Reinforces case law. Subject to any agreement to the contrary, the person making the contract is personally liable.

Phonogram Ltd. v Lane – Promoter who accepted money on behalf of an unformed company was liable to return it when company not formed.

Protection for the promoter:

- postpone finalising contracts until company is formed
- enter agreement of novation or assign the contract
- buy an 'off the shelf' company, so it is ready to contract
- include term in contract giving company the right to sue under Contracts (Rights of Third Parties) Act 1999
- agree no personal liability for the promoter.

Registration

The following documents must be submitted to the Registrar in order to form a company:

Memorandum of association – Signed by all subscribers and stating that they wish to form a company and agree to become members of the company.
Application – The application form must include the proposed name of the company, whether the members will have limited liability (by shares or guarantee), whether the company is to be private or public and details of the registered office.
Articles – The model articles apply if no articles are supplied.
Statement of capital and initial shareholdings – This must state the number of shares, their aggregate nominal value, how much has been unpaid and a contact address for each subscriber.
Statement of guarantee (if applicable) – This states the maximum amount each member undertakes to contribute.
Statement of consent to act – The company confirms that the director or secretary has given their consent to act.
Statement of compliance – This provides confirmation that CA06 has been complied with. It may be made in paper or electronic form.
Registration fee

Public companies	Registrar's duties
In order to obtain a trading certificate, public companies must additionally state: • Nominal value of allotted share capital ≥ £50,000. • At least ¼ nominal value and all premium paid. • Amount of preliminary expenses and any benefits given to promoters.	• **Inspect documents** and ensure Companies Act requirements fulfilled. • **Issue certificate of incorporation** which is conclusive evidence that Companies Act requirements fulfilled. Company exists from date on certificate of incorporation. • **Issue trading certificate** to public companies: s761.
If no trading certificate: • **Criminal offence to carry on business**, but contracts still binding on company. • **Directors personally liable** if company defaults within 21 days of due date.	

Streamlined company registration

The Streamlined Company Registration Service allows for new businesses to register their company and also register for tax at the same time. This makes it easier for new businesses to fulfil their legal obligations by registering with Companies House and HMRC at the same time.

Name of company

- Must have limited (Ltd) or public limited company (plc) at end if applicable.
- Cannot be same as another in index of names.
- Cannot use certain words which are illegal or offensive.
- Must have Secretary of State's consent to use certain words e.g. 'England', 'Chartered'.

The Secretary of State can force a company to change its name in the following circumstances.

Reason	Period
The name is the same as, or too like, an existing registered name.	12 months
The name gives so misleading an indication of the nature of the company's activities as to be likely to cause harm to the public.	No time limit
Misleading information or undertakings were given when applying for a name that required approval.	5 years

Articles of association

The articles form the company's internal constitution. They:

- Set out the manner in which the company is to be governed, and
- Regulate the relationship between the company and its shareholders.

Contents of Articles

Single document with consecutively numbered paragraphs.

Covers important areas such as:

- Appointment and dismissal of directors
- Powers, responsibilities and liabilities of directors
- Directors' meetings
- Members' rights
- Dividends
- Communication with members
- Issue of shares
- Documents and records

Model articles

For companies incorporated under CA06, model articles have been prescribed by the Secretary of State.

These model articles apply where a company is formed without registering articles or where the articles registered do not exclude or modify the model articles.

A company:

- may adopt the model articles in full or in part;
- is deemed to have adopted the model articles if there is no express or implied provision to exclude them; or
- may draft its own unique Articles.

Entrenchment

It is possible to entrench some of the articles. This means that a specified procedure (e.g. unanimous consent) may be required to change them.

Alteration of Articles	Contractual effect of articles
<ul><li>s21 CA06 – by **special resolution** (75% majority).</li><li>Must be '**bona fide in interests of company as a whole**':<ul><li>for members to decide</li><li>court will not interfere unless no reasonable man would consider bona fide</li><li>if bona fide – immaterial that happens to inflict hardship or has retrospective operation</li><li>will be void if actual fraud/oppression.</li></ul></li><li>Not invalid merely because causes breach of contract – but that does not excuse breach.</li></ul>**Southern Foundries Ltd. v Shirlaw** – MD could sue for breach of contract when articles amended to enable him to be removed.	The articles bind the company and its members to the same extent as if there were covenants on the part of the company and of each member to observe those provisions: S33 CA06. Case law shows that the articles are a contract binding:<ul><li>company to its members – **Hickman v Kent or Romney Marsh Sheepbreeders Association**.</li><li>members to the company – **Pender v Lushington**.</li><li>members to one another – **Rayfield v Hands**.</li></ul>Note: Articles are not a contract binding the company to non-members – **Eley v Positive Government Security Life Assurance**, and they do not bind the members in any other capacity – **Beattie v E F Beattie**.

Registers

Register of	Contents
Members	Names, addresses, date became/ceased, number of shares, type, amount paid up.
Directors (and company secretary, if applicable)	Name, occupation, nationality, other directorships within the last five years and date of birth. Should now contain service addresses rather than details of the directors' residential addresses. The service address can be simply 'the company's registered office'. The residential addresses will be withheld from the public register. However, they will remain available to the Registrar and certain specified public bodies and credit reference agencies.
Charges	Name of chargee, type of charge, property charged, amount and date created.
Persons with significant control	Details of name, service address, residential address, country and state of residence, nationality, date of birth, date they became a PSC and the nature of company control.
Resolutions and meetings	Records must be kept for a minimum period of 10 years.

The **Registers** must normally be **kept at** the company's **registered office** (although the register of members can be kept where it is made up) and must be a**vailable for public inspection**.

Under the SBEEA 2015 private companies can opt out of maintaining separate private registers and instead keep certain information on the public register at Companies House.

Requests for inspection must provide details about the person seeking the information, the purpose of the request and whether the information will be disclosed to others. The company may apply to the court for an order that it need not comply with the request.

Accounting records and annual return

Accounting records	Annual confirmation statement

Must contain:
• details of all money received and spent
• record of assets and liabilities
• statement of stocks at end of year
• statements of all goods sold and purchased, showing goods and the buyers and sellers (except in the retail trade).
	• Must be filed with Companies House which states that the company has provided all of the information it was required to provide within the previous 12 months.
	• Provided within 14 days of expiry of the previous 12 month period. For new companies, the first statement should be provided 12 months from the date of incorporation of the company.
	• Confirm changes to:
	  – address of registered office
	  – type of company
	  – principal business activities
	  – details of officers
	  – details of issued shares and their holders
	  – details of private company elections to dispense with holding AGMs/laying accounts.

Annual financial statements

- Balance sheet/statement of financial position and profit and loss account/statement of comprehensive income showing true and fair view.
- Directors' report stating amount of dividend and likely future developments.
- Laid before general meeting and copy filed with Registrar.

chapter 8

Capital and financing

In this chapter

- Types of shares.
- Class rights.
- Share capital – terminology.
- Issuing shares.
- Capital maintenance.
- Distributions.
- Debentures.
- Fixed v floating charges.
- Loan capital v share capital.

Types of shares

	Preference shares	Ordinary shares (equity)
Voting rights	None, or restricted by the articles of association.	Full.
Dividend rights	Fixed dividend paid in priority to other dividends, usually cumulative.	Paid after preference dividend. Not fixed.
Surplus on winding up	Prior return of capital, but cannot participate in any surplus.	Entitled to share surplus assets after repayment of preference shares.

Class rights

The special rights attached to each class such as dividend rights, distribution of capital on a winding up and voting.

The procedure for varying class rights depends on whether any procedure is specified in the articles:

Is procedure to vary specified?	Method of variation
Yes	Procedure set out in articles must be followed.
No	Variation needs special resolution or written consent of 75% in nominal value of the class: s630 CA06.

White v Bristol Aeroplane – Bonus issue is not a variation of class rights.

Greenhalgh v Arderne Cinemas – Subdivision of shares is not a variation of class rights.

Minority protection (s633 CA06)

- Holders of 15% of nominal value of class
- who did not consent to the variation
- may ask court to cancel within 21 days of the passing of the resolution.

Share capital – terminology

Issued share capital	Issued share capital comprises share capital that has actually been issued, released or sold by the company.
Paid up share capital	The amount which shareholders have actually paid on the shares issued.
Called up share capital	The amount of unpaid share capital which has been called for from shareholders but not yet paid.
Uncalled share capital	The amount of unpaid share capital that has not yet been called for from shareholders and therefore also remains unpaid.
Statutory pre-emption rights	New shares are offered to existing shareholders in proportion to their existing shareholding. Raises new funds. Purpose is not to dilute individual member shareholding.

Bonus issues	Carried out by using some of the company's reserves to issue fully paid shares to existing shareholders in proportion to their shareholdings.
	Do not raise any new funds.
	Also referred to as scrip or capitalisation issue.
Rights issues	New shares offered to existing shareholders in proportion to their shareholdings.
	Raise new funds.
	Shares usually offered at discount to current market value (but not at discount to nominal value).

Issuing shares

Authority	Issue at a premium
- The directors need authority in order to allot shares. - This may be given by the articles, or by passing an ordinary resolution. - The authority must state the maximum number of shares to be allotted and the expiry date for the authority (maximum five years).	S610 CA06 requires any premium to be credited to a share premium account, which may only be used for: - writing off the expenses of the issue of those shares - writing off any commission paid on the issue of those shares - issuing bonus shares.
Issue at a discount	**Paying for shares – public companies**
- Can't issue shares at discount on nominal value: s580 CA06. - **Breach** – issue still valid but allottee must pay up the discount plus interest. - Can issue debentures at a discount if don't have immediate right to convert to shares.	- Subscribers must pay cash for their subscription shares. - Payment for shares must not be in the form of work or services. - Shares cannot be allotted until at least one-quarter of their nominal value and the whole of any premium have been paid. - Non-cash consideration must be received within five years. - Non-cash consideration must be independently valued.

Capital maintenance

The capital of a limited company is regarded as a 'buffer fund' for creditors.

The rules on maintenance of capital exist to prevent a company reducing its capital by returning it to its members, whether directly or indirectly. This means that, as a general rule, a limited company cannot reduce its share capital or purchase its own shares. There are, however, some exceptions to this general rule.

Reduction of capital

Under s641 CA06, a company can reduce its capital at any time, for any reason.

- Reduce/cancel liabilities on partly paid shares; i.e. company gives up claim for money owing.
- Return capital in excess of company's needs; i.e. company reduces assets by repaying cash to shareholders.
- Cancel paid-up capital no longer represented by assets; i.e. company has debit balance on reserves. It writes this off by reducing capital and thereby does not need to make good past losses.

Capital and financing

Procedure for public companies:

- Pass a special resolution.

- Apply to the court to confirm the special resolution.

- If reduction involves one of the first two methods above, court must require company to settle a list of creditors entitled to object.

- The court must not confirm the reduction until it is satisfied that all creditors have either consented to the reduction or had their debts discharged or secured.

- The company must file documents with the Registrar. If the share capital of a public company falls below £50,000, it must re-register as a private company.

Simplified procedure for private companies:

- Pass a special resolution supported by a solvency statement.

- The solvency statement is a statement by each of the directors that the company will be able to meet its debts within the following year.

- A solvency statement made without reasonable grounds is an offence punishable by fine and/or imprisonment.

- Copies of the resolution, solvency statement and a statement of capital must be filed with the Registrar within 15 days.

Treasury shares

Created when a company purchases its own shares from distributable profits. The shares do not have to be cancelled so 10% of the shares can be held 'in treasury' which means they can be re-issued without the usual formalities.

Distributions

Company can only make distribution (e.g. pay dividend) out of distributable profits.	The company declares a dividend by passing an ordinary resolution. The amount paid cannot exceed the amount recommended by directors.

Distributable profits = accumulated realised profits less accumulated realised losses (s830 CA06).
• Profit/loss – trading or capital.
• Accumulated – overall profit/loss, not just one year in isolation.
• Realised:
  – not revaluation
  – provisions (e.g. depreciation, bad debts) deemed realised.
	Undistributable reserves
	• Share premium account.
	• Capital redemption reserve (Used only for bonus issues).
	• Unrealised profits (i.e. revaluation reserve).
	• Reserves the company is forbidden to distribute.

Plcs can only declare dividend if net assets will not fall below total of called up share capital and undistributable reserves. Use latest audited accounts to calculate.	**Consequences of unlawful dividend** • Directors liable to make good loss. • Shareholders who knew/had reasonable grounds to know must repay. • Auditors liable if paid in reliance on eroneous accounts.

Debentures

Definition

A debenture is a document issued by a company containing an acknowledgment of its indebtedness whether charged on the company's assets or not.

All trading companies have implied power to borrow for purpose of business.

Advantages of debentures	Disadvantages of debentures
• Board does not (generally) need authority of general meeting to issue debentures. • As debentures carry no votes they do not dilute/affect control of company. • Interest chargeable against profit before tax. • May be cheaper to service than shares. • No restrictions on issuing at a discount or on redemption.	• Interest must be paid out of pre-tax profits, irrespective of profits of company. If necessary must be paid out of capital. • Default may precipitate liquidation and/or administration if secured. • High gearing will affect share price.

Fixed v floating charges

Fixed charge	Floating charge
A fixed charge is a legal or equitable mortgage on a specific asset (e.g. land), which prevents the company dealing with the asset without the consent of the mortgagee.	A floating charge is an equitable charge on a class of assets present and future that will change from time to time and which company can use without the chargee's consent (e.g. stock): **Re Yorkshire Woolcombers Association**.
A fixed charge has three main characteristics: • it is on an identified asset • the asset is intended to be retained permanently in the business • the company has no general freedom to deal with (e.g. sell) the asset.	A floating charge has three main characteristics: • it is on a class of assets, present and future • the assets within the class will change from time to time • the company has freedom to deal with the charged assets in the ordinary course of its business.

Advantages and disadvantages	Crystallisation
Advantages of floating charge to company Company can deal freely with the assets. Wider class of assets can be charged. **Disadvantages of floating charge to chargee** Value of security uncertain until crystallises. Lower priority than fixed charge. Liquidator can ignore if created within 12 months preceding a winding up. This is to prevent a company from giving preference to one of its unsecured creditors by giving a floating charge over its assets.	A floating charge does not attach to any particular asset until crystallisation. **Crystallisation** means the company can no longer deal freely with the assets. It occurs in following cases: • liquidation • company ceases to carry on business • any event specified (e.g. company unable to pay debts; company fails to look after property; company fails to maintain stock levels).
Priority	**Registration**
• Equal charges – first created has priority. • Fixed charge – priority over floating charge. • An unregistered registerable charge has no priority over a registered charge. Can prohibit creation of later charge with priority, but only effective if subsequent chargee has notice of prohibition as well as charge.	Notify **Registrar** within **21 days** of creation. **Failure:** • renders charge void against liquidator • fine on company and every officer in default • money secured becomes immediately repayable. **Who can register?** The company or the chargeholder.

Loan capital v share capital

	Loan capital	Share capital
Definition	A debenture is a document issued by a company containing an acknowledgment of its indebtedness.	A share is the interest of a shareholder in a company measured by a sum of money.
Voting rights	A creditor of the company, therefore no voting rights.	A member (owner) of the company, therefore voting rights depending on class of shares.
Income	Contractual right to interest irrespective of availability of profits.	Dividends depend on availability of profits.
Liquidation	Priority with respect to repayment.	Receive repayment after creditors, but can participate in surplus assets.
Maintenance of capital	Does not need to be maintained.	Must be maintained.

chapter

Directors

In this chapter

- Types of director.
- Appointment.
- Disqualification.
- Removal.
- Directors duties.
- Statutory controls over directors.
- Authority of directors.

Types of director

Director	'Any person occupying the position of director by whatever name called': s250 CA06. The decision as to whether someone is a director is therefore based on their function, not their title.
De Jure Director	A person who is formally and legally appointed or elected as director in accordance with the articles of association of the company and gives written consent to hold the office of a director.
De Facto Director	A person who is not a de jure director but performs the acts or duties of a director.
Managing director/chief executive	The model articles allow the board to delegate to the MD any powers they see fit. MD has dual role – member of board and also executive officer. **Freeman & Lockyer v Buckhurst Park Properties** – the MD has the apparent authority to enter into all contracts of a commercial nature.
Shadow director	'A person in accordance with whose directions or instructions the directors of the company are accustomed to act': s251 CA06. Not a shadow director if advice is given only in a professional capacity.

Executive director	Likely to be a full-time employee involved in management. Contract must be available for inspection by members.
Non-executive director	Part-time. Brings outside expertise to board. Not an employee. Exerts control over executive directors.
Chairman of board	Chairs meetings of board. Acts as spokesman for the company. Has a casting vote.
Alternate Director	Appointed by a director to attend and vote for them at board meetings which they are unable to attend.

Appointment

First directors	• Minimum: public = two; private = one. • Maximum – no statutory maximum, but articles may specify.
Appointment procedure	• Usually appointed by the existing directors or by ordinary resolution. • A director's actions are valid notwithstanding that his appointment was defective: s161 CA06.
Model articles for public companies	• First AGM all retire and offer themselves for re-election by ordinary resolution. • Each AGM one third retire (most senior). Can be re-elected. • Casual vacancies are filled by board until next AGM when must stand for election.
Publicity	Notify Companies House within 14 days of new appointments and any changes in particulars. Also enter details in Register of Directors.
Service contracts	• Cannot exceed two years unless they have been approved by the shareholders by ordinary resolution: s188 CA06. • Directors of a quoted company must prepare a directors remuneration report for each financial year of the company. • Must be kept open for inspection at the registered office.
Compensation for loss of office	• Gratuitous payments must be disclosed to all members and approved by ordinary resolution.

Disqualification

Model articles	Vacate office if become bankrupt or insane.
Company Directors (Disqualification) Act 1986	
Effect of court order	Cannot be concerned in management of company directly/indirectly or act as liquidator, receiver or promoter. Maximum 15 years, unless otherwise stated.
Grounds for disqualification	• Convicted of serious offence in connection with management of company. • Persistent breach of CA06 – e.g. failure to file returns – maximum 5 years. • Fraudulent or wrongful trading. • An investigation by the Department for Business and Trade has held unfit to be concerned in management of company.
Breach of disqualification order	• Criminal offence (fine and imprisonment). • Personally liable for debts of company while so acting.

Directors

Removal

- Special notice (28 days) of resolution by persons wishing to remove director. The company must forward a copy of the resolution to the director concerned.

- Notice of meeting to director and all members entitled to attend and vote.

- Director can require company to circulate written representations to members.

- At the meeting, director can read out representations if no time for prior circulation. Director must be allowed to attend and speak. Ordinary resolution: s168 CA06.

Directors duties

S171	Duty to act within powers. **Hogg v Cramphorn**
S172	Duty to promote the success of the company.
S173	Duty to exercise independent judgement.
S174	Duty to exercise reasonable care, skill and diligence. An objective and a subjective test. **Dorchester Finance Co Ltd v Stebbing**
S175	Duty to avoid conflicts of interest. **IDC v Cooley**
S176	Duty not to accept benefits from third parties. **Boston Deep Sea Fishing & Ice Co v Ansell**
S177	Duty to declare interest in proposed transaction or arrangement. **Aberdeen Railway v Blakie**

Directors

Breach of directors' duties

Duties are owed to the company as a whole, not to individual members:
Percival v Wright (1902).
Breach of duty may carry the following consequences:

- The director may be required to make good any loss suffered by the company.
- Contracts entered into between the company and the director may be rendered voidable.
- Any property taken by the director from the company can be recovered from him if still in his possession.
- Property may be recovered directly from a third party, unless that third party acquired it for value and in good faith.
- An injunction may be an appropriate remedy where the breach has not yet occurred.

S239 CA06 states that the company can ratify a breach of duty by passing an ordinary resolution.

Statutory controls over directors

Certain matters require the approval of members in a general meeting in order to be valid.

S188 CA 06: Directors' service contracts	Where contract lasts for more than 2 years it must be approved by the members.
S190 CA 06: Substantial property transactions	Where a director acquires from the company (or vice versa) a substantial non-cash asset.
S197 CA 06: Loans to directors	Any loans given to directors, or guarantees provided as security for loans provided to directors, must be approved by members.
S217 CA 06: Non-contractual payments to directors	Any non-contractual payment to directors for loss of office must be approved by the members.

Authority of directors

Express	• Where authority is expressly given, all decisions taken are binding.
Implied	• Authority flows from a person's position.
	• The person appointed as the managing director has the implied authority to bind the company in the same way as the board.
	• The MD/CEO is assumed to have all powers usually exercised by an MD/CEO.
Apparent/ Ostensible	• Such authority arises where a director is held out by the other board members as having the authority to bind the company.
	• If a third party acts on such a representation, the company is estopped from denying its truth **(Freeman & Lockyer v Buckhurst Park Properties)**.

chapter 10

Corporate administration

In this chapter

- Company secretary.
- Auditor.
- Duties, resignation and removal.
- Types of meeting.
- Who can call a meeting?
- Notice.
- Resolutions.
- Procedure at meetings.

Company secretary

- Every public company must have a secretary. Private companies are not obliged to have a secretary.
- Secretary of public company must be qualified:
  - held office of company secretary in plc for at least 3 out of preceding 5 years or
  - is a solicitor, barrister or member of ICAEW, ACCA, CIMA, ICSA, CIPFA or
  - by virtue of other position/qualification appears capable.
- The secretary is usually appointed and removed by the directors.

Duties	Authority to bind company in contract
<ul><li>Documentation in order, returns made to Registrar and registers kept.</li><li>Notice and minutes of meetings.</li><li>Countersigning documents to which company seal affixed.</li></ul>	<ul><li>Actual.</li><li>Implied re contracts of administrative nature:</li></ul>**Panorama Development v Fidelis Furnishing Fabrics** Company secretary ordered services for his own, not company's, use. Held that the contract was binding on the company as the contract was of the sort a company secretary should be able to carry out.

Auditor

Appointment	
• Generally appointed by the shareholders by ordinary resolution, but directors can appoint first auditor and fill casual vacancies. • Qualifications – member of Recognised Supervisory Body and eligible under rules. • Must not be – officer/employee of company or partner of officer/employee.	• A company must inform the Secretary of State if it has failed to appoint. The Secretary of State then has powers to appoint.

Duties, resignation and removal

Removal	Duties
By **ordinary resolution with special notice** at a general meeting. (Cannot remove by written resolution). **Resignation** • May resign by **written notice** to company. • Auditor **may require directors to call meeting within 28 days** if there are circumstances connected with resignation.	**Statutory duty** to report to the members on whether the accounts: • give a true and fair view and • have been properly prepared in accordance with the Companies Act and the relevant financial reporting framework. Investigate and form an opinion as to whether: • proper books of accounting records have been kept, and proper returns adequate for their audit have been received from branches not visited by them • the accounts are in agreement with the books of account and returns. **Powers** • Receive notice of, attend and speak at general meetings. • Access to books, accounts, vouchers. • Require information/explanations from officers and employees. (Criminal offence to fail to provide information requested, unless not reasonably practicable to do so).

Types of meeting

Annual general meeting

Timing	Public companies must hold an AGM within the six months following their financial year end: s336. Private companies are not required to hold an AGM.
Failure to hold	The company and every officer in default can be fined if an AGM is not held. Any member can apply to the Department for Business and Trade to convene the meeting.
Notice	**21 days' notice** is required unless every member entitled to attend and vote agrees to a shorter period. Must state that the meeting is an AGM.
Business	Usual business includes consider accounts, appoint auditors, elect directors and declare dividends.
Resolutions	Members holding at least 5% of the voting rights (or at least 100 members holding on average £100 paid-up capital) have the right to propose a resolution and require the company to circulate details to all members. If the request is received before the financial year end, the members are not required to cover the costs of circulation. Otherwise, the members requesting the statement must deposit a sum to cover the company's costs.

General meeting

Timing	Held whenever required. Must be held by a plc if a serious loss of capital has occurred, i.e. net assets have fallen to less than half of the paid up share capital.
Notice	At least **14 days**.
Business	The person who requisitions the meeting sets the agenda.

Class meeting

Purpose	Meeting of a class of shareholders, usually to consider a variation of their class rights.
Procedure	Notice, etc as for general meetings.
Quorum	Two persons holding or representing by proxy at least 1/3 in nominal value of the issued shares of the class in question.

Who can call a meeting?

Directors	Articles usually delegate power to directors.
Members	• May require directors to call GM if hold 5% paid up voting capital. • Directors must call within 21 days of receiving requisition. • Meeting must take place within 28 days of the notice convening the meeting. • If the directors do not call a meeting, the members who requested the meeting (or any members holding over 50% of the total voting rights) may themselves call a meeting to take place within three months of the initial request and recover their expenses from the company.
Resigning auditor	May require directors to convene so he can explain the reasons for his resignation.
Court	On application of director/member where otherwise impracticable, e.g. to break a deadlock.

Notice

Who must receive notice?	Every member and every director: s310.
Failure to give notice	Accidental failure to give notice to one or more persons does not invalidate the meeting: s313.
Contents of notice	Date, time and place of the meeting. The general nature of the business to be transacted. The text of any special resolutions.
Length of notice period	**AGM – 21 days** Less if every member entitled to attend and vote agrees. **GM – 14 days** Less if members holding at least 95% of shares agree. (Where company is private, can be reduced to 90%).
Special notice	Requires 28 days' notice. Required for the removal of a director or auditor.

Resolutions

Type:	% required to pass:	To Registrar?	Purpose of resolution:
Special	75	Yes – within 15 days	Alter name, objects or articles. Reduce share capital. Wind up company.
Ordinary	Simple Majority	Only if required by statute	Used whenever the law or the articles do not require a special resolution.
Written (private companies only)	Same majority as required in GM	Yes if 75% majority required	The purpose can be anything apart from resolutions requiring special notice. Members cannot revoke their agreement. The date of the resolution is the date when the necessary majority has been reached. The resolution must be passed within 28 days from its circulation.

Procedure at meetings

A **quorum** is the minimum number of members that needs to be present at a meeting in order to validate business. It is generally two persons; members or proxies: s318 CA06.

Voting is by a **show of hands** initially, unless a poll is demanded. A show of hands means one member one vote, irrespective of the number of shares held.

A **poll** may be demanded by members holding at least 10% of the total voting rights (or by not fewer than 5 members having the right to vote on the resolution). A poll means one vote per share. The result of a poll replaces the result of the previous show of hands.

Quoted companies must publish the results of polls on their website: s341 CA06.

Members have a statutory right under s324 CA06 to appoint one or more persons as their '**proxy**'. A proxy can attend meetings, vote and speak on behalf of the member for whom he is acting.

chapter 11

Insolvency

In this chapter

- Voluntary liquidation.
- Members' voluntary liquidation.
- Creditors' voluntary liquidation.
- Compulsory liquidation.
- Application of assets.
- Administration.

Voluntary liquidation: s.84 IA 86

When a voluntary liquidation may occur:

- Where period fixed for duration of company expires or an event occurs upon which the articles provide that a company should be wound up and an ordinary resolution passed.
- Special resolution passed.

Types of voluntary liquidation:

- Members' voluntary liquidiation – if company is solvent.
- Creditors' voluntary liquidation – if company is insolvent.

A members' voluntary liquidation must be converted in a creditors' voluntary liquidation if the liquidator discovers that the company's debts will not be paid in full.

Chapter 11

Members' voluntary liquidation

The directors make a declaration of solvency stating that they are of the opinion that the company will be able to pay its debts within 12 months. It is a criminal offence to make a false declaration.

Winding up commences from the date of passing of the appropriate resolution.

The members **appoint a named insolvency practitioner as liquidator**.

The liquidator is responsible for realising the assets and distributing the proceeds.

The liquidator presents his report to a **final meeting** of the members.

The liquidator **informs the Registrar** of the final meeting and submits a copy of his report.

The Registrar registers the report and the company is **dissolved three months later**.

Creditors' voluntary liquidation

- Winding up commences from the passing of the appropriate resolution (S86 IA 1986).

- The members appoint a liquidator. The directors must then deliver a notice to the creditors seeking their decision on the liquidator. The directors must also send to the creditors a **statement of affairs** within 7 working days.

- The creditors can approve the liquidator either by virtual meeting or by the 'deemed consent' process. Under this process, approval is deemed unless 10% of the creditors of the company raise objections to the proposed liquidator. The members and creditors may appoint up to five persons to serve on a **liquidation committee.**

- The liquidator is responsible for realising the assets and distributing the proceeds.

- The liquidator submits his final report to the members and creditors.

- The liquidator submits a copy of his report to the Registrar.

- The Registrar registers the report and the company is **dissolved three months later.**

Compulsory liquidation

Grounds for winding-up: s.122 IA86	Petitioners
• Company has passed **special resolution** to be wound up by the court. • Public co **hasn't been issued with trading certificate within a year** of registration. • Company has **not commenced business within a year** of being incorporated. • The company is **unable to pay its debts**. • It is **just and equitable** to wind up.	• The company itself. • The Official Receiver. • The Department for Business and Trade. • A contributory = any person who is liable to contribute to the assets of the company when it is being wound up (contributory must prove that the company is solvent). • A creditor owed at least £750. **Effect of winding-up** • All actions for the recovery of debt against the company are stopped. • Company ceases to carry on business except where it is necessary for winding up. • Powers of directors cease. • Employees automatically made redundant.

Application of assets

The liquidator must repay debts in the following order.

- Fixed charge-holders.
- Expenses of liquidation.
- Preferential creditors.
- Secondary preferential creditors - HMRC in respect of VAT, PAYE income tax and employee's NIC.
- Floating charge-holders.
- Unsecured creditors – rank equally amongst themselves.
- Post-liquidation interest.
- Members – declared but unpaid dividends.
- Members – return of capital.
- Any surplus to be distributed to members.

Administration

Purposes	Consequences of administration
• Rescue a company in financial difficulty. • Achieve a better result for the creditors than would be likely if the company were to be wound up. • Realise property to pay one or more secured creditors. **Who can appoint an administrator?** • The **court** in response to a petition by e.g. a creditor. • The **holder of a floating charge**. • The company or its directors provided that winding up has not already begun.	• The rights of creditors to enforce debts remain suspended. • All company documents must state that company is in administration and the name of the administrator. • Any petition for winding up is dismissed. • No resolution may be passed to wind up the company. • A qualified insolvency practitioner is appointed to administer the affairs of the company.

Carrying out the administration	Ending the administration

• Administrator must send a **statement of proposals** to all creditors and members.
• The proposals must be approved by the creditors of the company. This approval can be given by:
  • Deemed consent process
  • Virtual meeting
  • Some other reasonable method.
• The creditors have the right to form a creditors meeting of between 3 to 5 creditors. If formed the administrator must hold a meeting of the creditors within 6 weeks of its establishment.
• If the creditors do not approve the proposals, the court may dismiss the administrator or make such provisions as it sees fit.
• If the creditors approve the proposals, the administrator can carry them out.
	• The administrator may apply to the court for discharge at any time. He must make an application when the purpose of the order has been achieved or is incapable of being achieved.
	• The administration must be **completed within 12 months** of the date on which it commenced. This term can be extended with consent of the court or the creditors.

chapter 12

Corporate and fraudulent behaviour

In this chapter

- Insider dealing.
- Market abuse.
- Money laundering.
- Bribery.
- Fraud.
- Failure to prevent fraud.
- Failure to prevent tax evasion.
- Fraudulent and wrongful trading.

Insider dealing

Legislation	Contained in **Part V Criminal Justice Act 1993**.
The offences	An individual who has information as an insider is guilty of insider dealing if: • they **deal in securities** that are price-affected in relation to the information • they **encourage another person to deal** (knowing or having reasonable cause to believe that dealing would take place) • they **disclose the information** (otherwise than in the proper performance of the functions of their employment, office or profession).
Insider	A person has information as an insider if it is, and he knows that it is, inside information or he has it, and knows that he has it, from an inside source.
Inside information	Inside information is information which: • **relates to particular securities** or to a particular issuer of securities • **is specific** or precise • has **not** been made **public** • if made public would be likely to have a **significant effect on the price**.

| Inside source | A person has information from an inside source if and only if:
- he has it through being a director, employee, or shareholder of an issuer of securities ('primary insider')
- he has it through having access to the information by virtue of his employment, office or profession ('primary insider')
- he has the information from a person who is within either of these categories ('secondary insider'). |
|---|---|
| Defences | - Didn't expect the dealing to result in a profit (or the avoidance of a loss) attributable to the fact that the information in question was price-sensitive.
- Believed on reasonable grounds that the information had been widely disclosed.
- Would have done what he did even if he had not had the information. |
| Consequences | Imprisonment (6 months' summary or 10 years' indictment) and a fine.

Transactions remain valid and enforceable. No civil compensation.

Director breaches fiduciary duty and is liable to account for any profit made. |

Market abuse

Legislation	The Financial Services and Markets Act 2000
Behaviour	Seven types of behaviour amounts to market abuse: • Insider dealing • Improper disclosure • Misuse of information • Manipulating transactions • Manipulating devices • Dissemination • Distortion and misleading behaviour
Consequences	Unlimited fine and a public reprimand by the Financial Conduct Authority

Money laundering

Definition	Money laundering is the process by which the proceeds of crime are converted into assets which appear to have a legal rather than an illegal source.
Legislation	**Proceeds of Crime Act 2002**
Phases	- **Placement** – the initial disposal of the proceeds of criminal activity into an apparently legitimate business activity or property. - **Layering** – the transfer of money from business to business, or place to place, in order to conceal its initial source. - **Integration** – the culmination of the previous procedures through which the money takes on the appearance of coming from a legitimate source.
Offences	- Laundering – concealing, disguising, or transferring criminal property. - Failure to report – individuals (such as accountants and solicitors) may be guilty of an offence of failing to disclose knowledge or suspicion of money laundering where they know or suspect, or have reasonable grounds for knowing or suspecting, that another person is engaged in laundering the proceeds of crime. - Tipping off – making a disclosure likely to prejudice an investigation.
Penalties	Money laundering – maximum 14 years' imprisonment. Failure to report – maximum of five years' imprisonment and/or a fine. Tipping off – maximum of two years' imprisonment and/or a fine.

Bribery

Definition	It is the offering, giving, receiving, or soliciting of any item of value to influence the actions of an official or other person in charge of a public or legal duty.
Legislation	The Bribery Act 2010
Offences	• Bribing a person to induce or reward them to perform a relevant function improperly. • Requesting, accepting or receiving a bribe as a reward for performing a relevant function improperly. • Using a bribe to influence a foreign official to gain a business advantage. • A new form of corporate liability for failing to prevent bribery on behalf of a commercial organisation.
Defence	To have in place 'adequate procedures' to prevent bribery.
Penalties	• For individuals is a maximum sentence of 10 years. • For commercial organisations there maybe an unlimited fine.

Fraud

Legislation	The Fraud Act 2006
Offences	The defendant must have been dishonest, and have intended to make a gain or to cause loss to anther and have carried out one of the following: • fraud by making a false or misleading representation • fraud by failing to disclose information • fraud by abuse of position.

Failure to prevent fraud

Legislation	**The Economic Crime and Corporate Transparency Act 2023**
Offences	An employee, agent, subsidiary or other 'associated person' commits a fraud which benefits the organisation or its customers. Applies to large incorporated organisations and partnerships both inside and outside the UK, which meet two of the following criteria: • More than 250 employees • More than £36 million annual turnover • More than £18 million total balance sheet assets
Defence	Reasonable fraud prevention procedures in place.
Penalties	An unlimited fine.

Failure to prevent tax evasion

Legislation	The Criminal Finances Act 2017
Offences	A corporate offence on failure to prevent the criminal facilitation of criminal tax evasion. The offence can make a 'relevant body' criminally liable if it fails to prevent the facilitation of UK or non-UK tax evasion by an employee or 'associated person'. The offence applies to both UK and non-UK companies. An 'associated person' can be an individual, corporate entity or an employee of a corporate associated person, carrying out services on behalf of the 'relevant body'. A 'relevant body' is defined in the act as a company or a partnership.
Defence	At the time of the offence the relevant body had reasonable prevention procedures in place to prevent tax evasion facilitation offences or where it is unreasonable to expect such procedures.
Penalties	An unlimited fine for the relevant body and potential reputational damage.

Fraudulent and wrongful trading

	Fraudulent trading	**Wrongful trading**
Definition	Fraudulent trading occurs where the company's business is **carried on with intent to defraud** creditors or for any fraudulent purpose: s213 IA 1986. Note high burden of proof involved in proving dishonesty.	On winding-up it appears to court that company has gone into insolvent liquidation and, before start of winding up, director knew or ought to have concluded there was no **reasonable prospect that company could avoid insolvent liquidation**: S.214 IA 1986.
Who is liable?	Any persons knowingly party to the carrying on of the business.	Directors and shadow directors.
Consequences	• Contribute to company's assets. • 15 years' disqualification under CDDA86. • Fine and/or imprisonment.	• Contribute to company's assets. • 15 years' disqualification under CDDA86.
Case law	**R v Grantham** – ordering goods on credit knowing that they would not be paid for. Held: fraudulent trading.	**Re Produce Marketing Consortium** – defence that took all reasonable steps to minimise loss to creditors.

Corporate and fraudulent behaviour

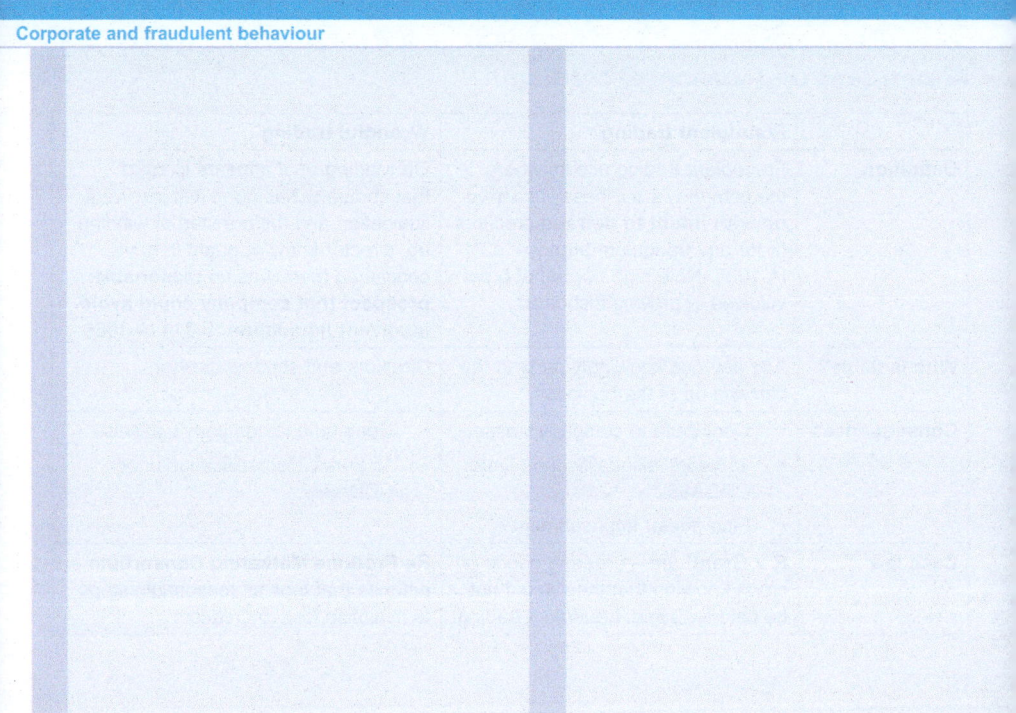

Index

Index

A

Acceptance 15
Adams v Lindsell 15
Adler v George 10
Administration 117
Agency 45
Articles 70
Auditor 103

B

Balfour v Balfour 20
Beattie v E F Beattie 72
Bettini v Gye 21
Breach of contract 25

C

Caparo Industries v Dickman 32
Capital maintenance 83
Capital redemption reserve 85
Carlill v Carbolic Smoke Ball Co 14, 15
Central London Property Trust v High Tree House 18
Chappell & Co. v Nestlé 17
Collins v Godefroy 17
Common law 7
Company Directors (Disqualification) Act 1986 95
Company secretary 102
Compulsory liquidation 115
Conditions 21
Consideration 16
Constructive dismissal 41
Corkery v Carpenter 10
Courts 4, 6, 9
Cox Toner (International) Ltd v Crook 41
Criminal law 1
Currie v Misa 16
Curtis v Chemical Cleaning 22

D

Damages 26
Debentures 83
Directors 91
Distributable profits 85
Distributions 83

Donoghue v Stevenson 30
Dunlop v Selfridge 16

E

Eley v Positive Government Security Life Assurance 72
Employment 35
Employment Rights Act 1996 42
Entores v Miles Far Eastern 15
Equity 7
Ewing v Buttercup Margarine Company 34

F

Felthouse v Bindley 15
Fisher v Bell 10, 14
Fixed charge 88
Floating charge 88
Fraudulent trading 127
Freeman & Lockyer v Buckhurst Park Properties 46, 92

G

Gibson v Manchester City Council 14
Gilford v Horne 58
Glasbrook Bros. v Glamorgan CC 17
Greenhalgh v Arderne Cinemas 79

H

Hadley v Baxendale 26
Hedley Byrne v Heller 32
Hickman v Kent or Romney Marsh Sheepbreeders Association 72
Hivac v Park Royal Scientific 37
Hollier v Rambler Motors 22
Household Fire Insurance v Grant 15
Human Rights Act 1998 6, 11
Hyde v Wrench 14

I

Innominate terms 21
Insolvency Act 1986 58
Intention to create legal relations 20
Interpretation 10

Index

J

JEB Fasteners v Marks, Bloom & Co. 32
Jones v Vernon's Pools 20
Judicial precedent 7, 8

K

Kelner v Baxter 66

L

Lee v Lee's Air Farming 57
Legislation 7
L'Estrange v Graucob 22
Limited Liability Partnership Regulations 2001 59
Limited Liability Partnerships 59
Limited Liability Partnerships Act 2000 51
Limited Partnership Act 1907 51
Loan capital 90

M

Macaura v Northern Life Assurance 57
Members' voluntary liquidation 113
Mendoza v Ghaidan 11

N

Name of company 69
Non-executive director 93
Notice 108

O

Obiter dicta 8
O'Brien v Associated Fire Alarms 41
Offer 14
Olley v Marlborough Court 22
Ordinary shares 78

P

Panorama Development v Fidelis Furnishing Fabrics 102
Partnership 61
Partnership Act 1890 51

Index

Part-payment problem 18
Partridge v Crittenden 14
Passing off 34
Pender v Lushington 72
Pepper v Webb 37
Pharmaceutical Society of GB v Boots 14
Phonogram Ltd v Lane 66
Photo Productions Ltd v Securicor 23
Postal rule 15
Poussard v Spiers 21
Preference shares 78
Pre-incorporation contracts 55, 66
Private company 55, 63
Promoters 55, 65
Public company 55, 63
Purchase of own shares 83

R

Ratio decidendi 8
Rayfield v Hands 72
Ready Mixed Concrete v Ministry of Pensions 36
Re Casey's Patents 16
Reduction of capital 83
Redundancy 42
Redundancy pay 43
Re-engagement 43
Registers 70, 73
Registration 55, 67
Reinstatement 43
Re McArdle 16
Re Produce Marketing Consortium 127
Resolutions 109
Re Yorkshire Woolcombers Association 88
R v Grantham 127

S

Salomon v Salomon & Co Ltd 57
Share capital 90
Share premium account 82
Simmonds v Dowty Seals Ltd 41
Simpkins v Pays 20
Southern Foundries Ltd v Shirlaw 72
Spurling v Bradshaw 22
Stilk v Myrick 17
Summary dismissal 38

Index

T

Terms 19
The Hansa Nord 21
Thomas v Thomas 17
Trading certificate 68
Twycross v Grant 65

U

UCTA 1977 24

V

Veil of incorporation 55, 57
Victoria Laundries v Newman 26
Voluntary liquidation 112

W

Warranties 21
Watteau v Fenwick 52
Western Excavating Ltd v Sharp 41
White v Bluett 17
White v Bristol Aeroplane 79
Williams v Roffey Bros 17
Woolfson v Strathclyde Regional Council 58
Wrongful trading 127

Y

Yewens v Noakes 36